Peter Pan CHILDREN'S BIBLE

"YOU HAVE SWORD AND SPEAR... I COME IN THE NAME OF THE LORD!"

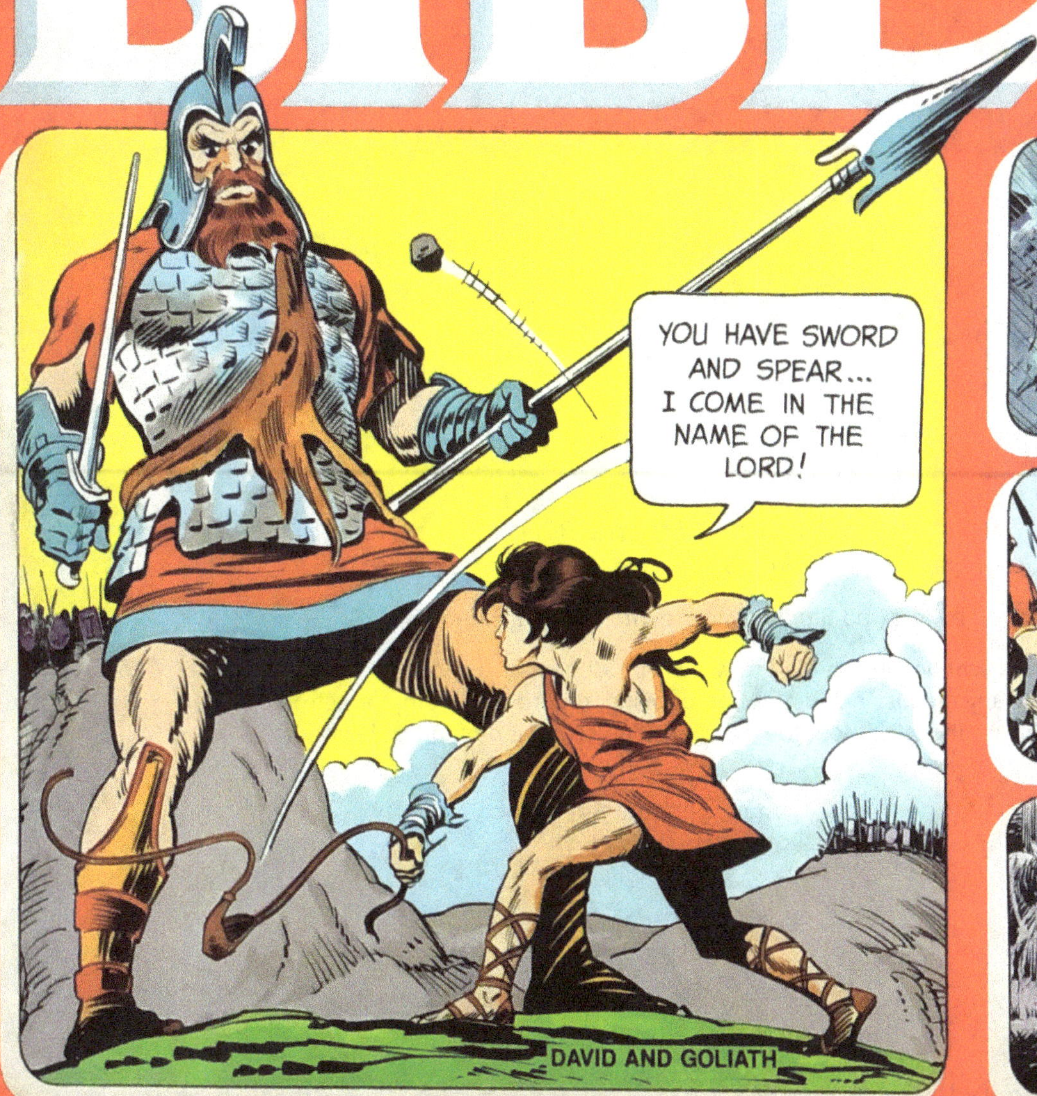

DAVID AND GOLIATH

NOAH'S ARK

SAMSON AND DELILAH

THE FIRST CHRISTMAS

The Peter Pan Children's Bible
Copyright ©2020 Inspired Studios Inc. All rights reserved.

Published by Inspired Studios, Inc, Boynton Beach, Florida 33473

No part of the publication or recording may be reproduced, distributed, or transmitted in any form or by any means, including photocopying, recording, or other electronic or mechanical methods, without the prior written permission of this publisher.

ISBN
Print 978-0-7396-3643-5
Digital 978-0-7396-3573-5

JACOB AND ESAU

In Canaan, the boy Isaac grew to manhood, remembering God's promise to Abraham, his father.

"Keep my laws, and I will bless you. Your people will be as many as the stars in heaven, and this land will be yours forever."

Isaac married late in life, and his wife Rebecca gave him twin sons -- Esau, who roamed the woods and became a mighty hunter -- and Jacob, who stayed at home and tended the flocks. Now Esau was Isaac's favorite. But Rebecca loved Jacob more -- and she hoped to see HIM the head of the family. Years passed -- and then, suddenly, it seemed the time had come...

...for Isaac had grown old, and blind -- and very feeble. And he sent for Esau, saying:

"My son -- I think I am dying."

"No, father -- no! You'll get well again -- I know it!"

"Esau -- listen: I have only a little time. So go now, and hunt down a deer for me -- and make me a stew of its meat, the way YOU know how to do it. And I will eat it and then, if God spares me, I will give you my final blessing. Go, my son."

"Yes, father."

Rebecca heard what Isaac said -- and she knew what it meant: if Isaac gave Esau his final blessing, then he would get everything Isaac owned -- and Jacob, her favorite, would get nothing. So she went to Jacob and commanded him to take a young goat from the flock, and kill it, and bring its meat to her for a stew.

"And you, Jacob -- you shall serve it to your father. And his blessing will be given not to Esau but to you!"

"But, mother, that isn't right. Besides, he'll see that it's me."

"Your father cannot see."

"But he'll touch my hand -- and then he'll know. Because Esau is hairy all over, and my skin is smooth."

"Do as I say, my son. Your father WILL take you for Esau -- I'll see to that! Now, here is all you have to do..."

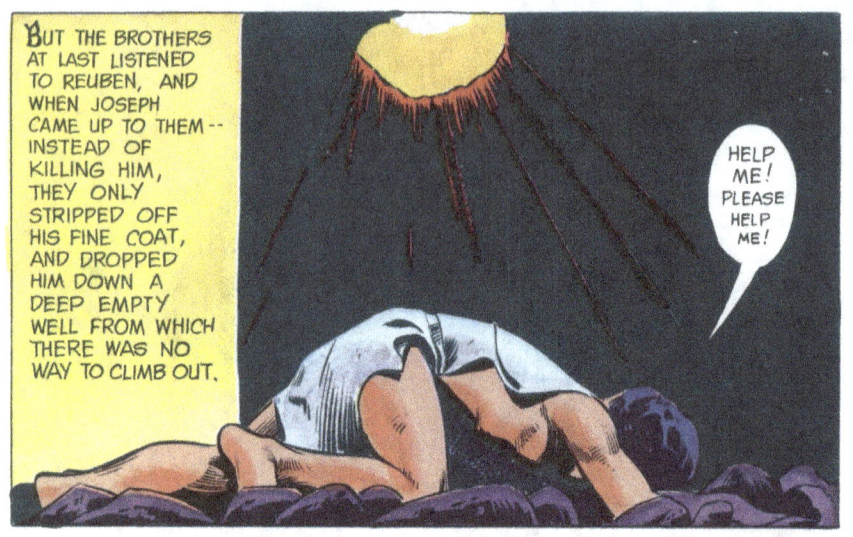

JOSEPH IN EGYPT

This is the story of Joseph of Canaan, who was stolen out of his homeland and was sold to Potiphar, a captain in the army of Pharaoh, ruler of Egypt. Now Joseph was a young man, as wise as he was handsome, for God was with him, and Potiphar was pleased with Joseph, and put him in charge of his household. But Potiphar's wife fell in love with Joseph, and when he would have nothing to do with her, she grew angry, and went to Potiphar, saying:

"Your slave has insulted me. Punish him!"

And Potiphar believed his wife, and Joseph was arrested, and thrown into prison, and time passed, and it seemed that God had turned his face away from Joseph, but it was not so. For one day, Pharaoh's chief steward was brought in as a prisoner -- because he had done some wrong. And this man became friends with Joseph, and one morning he said to him:

"I had a dream last night, Joseph -- and it worries me."

"Why?"

"Because I can't understand it. In Pharaoh's court, there were magicians who could have told me what it meant, but here..."

"Perhaps I can help you. Tell me your dream."

"Well... I dreamt I was a vine -- with three branches laden with grapes. Pharaoh's cup was in my hand, and I squeezed the grapes into the cup, and gave it to Pharaoh. Joseph, what do you make of it?"

"The three branches mean that in three days, Pharaoh will forgive you, and set you free."

And it was so. In three days, the steward was set free and restored to his place in the palace. Joseph remained in prison. Then one night, years later, Pharaoh himself was troubled by dreams, and his magicians were not able to explain them. Then the steward remembered Joseph, and he told Pharaoh, and Pharaoh said:

"Bring the Hebrew slave before me!"

And Joseph was brought forth out of prison, and Pharaoh said:

"Hear my dream -- and for your life, tell me what it means."

"By myself, I cannot. But God will give Pharaoh the answer."

"We will see. This was my dream. I was standing on the banks of a river, and seven fat cows came up and fed on the grass. Then seven thin cows came after them, and fell on the fat cows and ate them up. Later, I had another dream. I saw seven full ears of corn on one stalk -- and on another stalk, seven thin ears -- and the thin ears swallowed up the good ones. Well, Joseph?"

"God has shown Pharaoh what he is about to do."

"And what is that?"

"The seven fat cows and the seven full ears of corn mean that seven years of plenty are coming to Egypt. But the thin cows and the thin ears of corn mean that seven years of famine will follow the years of plenty. In that time the crops will fail, and many will die of hunger -- unless something is done to save them."

"How? What can be done?"

"Let Pharaoh see to it that in the years of plenty, a fifth part of all the food that grows in Egypt is set aside under your great seal -- and let the food be sold to all who need it when the lean years come."

And Pharaoh gave thought to the words of Joseph, and believed them, and he said: "Since God has shown you all this, YOU shall see it is done as you say. Behold, I give you power over all the land of Egypt, second only to mine!"

And Joseph went out over Egypt, and he gathered up a fifth part of all the grain that grew in the next seven years and stored it up in every city -- and then the lean years came, and the people hungered, and Joseph opened all the storehouses, and in Egypt there was bread. But it was not so in the countries nearby.

Because of the crop failure, Joseph's brothers came to Egypt to buy grain. Joseph recognized them. The reunion was an event of rejoicing as Joseph forgave them saying: "It was God who sent me ahead of you to Egypt to save men's lives." And Pharaoh rewarded Joseph by welcoming his family to live in Egypt and prosper. And God promised Jacob, Joseph's father, in a vision: "Do not be afraid to go to Egypt. I will make you a great nation."

ESCAPE FROM EGYPT

THE TEN COMMANDMENTS

SAMSON AND DELILAH

Samson was the strongest man in all the Promised Land. And it was well that he was strong. For in those days wild beasts roamed the country. Lions and bears came down from the mountains into the fields. One day, when Samson was working on his farm, a young lion sprang at him.

But Samson was so strong, he tore the lion apart with his hands.

But the people of Israel also had **MEN** for enemies.—The Philistines, a tribe of warriors on the western border of the land. Time and again, the Philistines would make their way into Israelite land and lay waste the towns. But the people of Israel wanted peace. They bound Samson up to offer him to the Philistines and brought him to Lehi.

The Philistines were many, and they carried spears. Samson had nothing—but the spirit of the Lord entered into Samson. His binding fell from his hands... and he picked up the jawbone of an ass and used it like a club against the Philistines, and slew many men.

And the Philistines swore that some day they would pay Samson back. Now this is how it came about. Samson fell in love with a woman—Delilah was her name. And the Philistines came to her, saying:

"We will pay you to help us."

"Help you... how?"

"Find out his secret. He has the strength of a hundred men. Why?"

"I don't know."

"Find out. We will pay you very well."

And so one night Delilah asked Samson, if he loved her to tell her the secret of his strength. At first he would not, but she asked again and again, and at last Samson said:

"The day I was born, my mother and father gave me to God. They swore, and then I swore, that I would drink no wine, and eat no unclean food—and never would I cut my hair. And because I have kept my word, God has given me great strength."

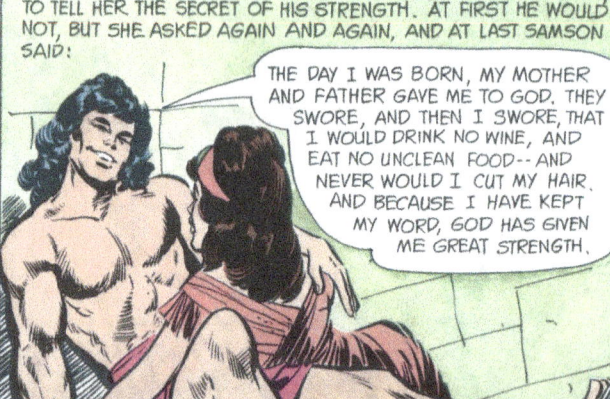

"So, if your head were shaved—"

"I would become as weak as you are!"

DAVID AND GOLIATH

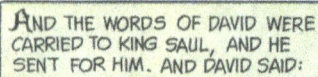

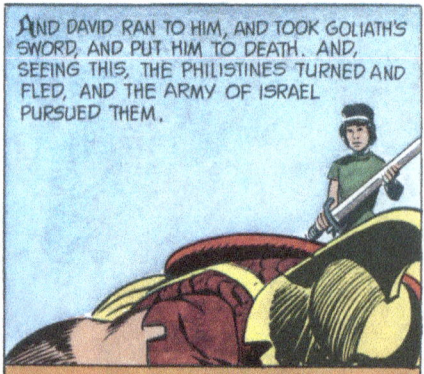

THE WISDOM OF SOLOMON

JONAH AND THE WHALE

DANIEL IN THE LION'S DEN

Now when Darius was King over Persia, he captured the great city of Babylon, and he chose three men to rule it in his name. One of the three was Daniel, an Israelite. Long years before, the Babylonians had conquered the Israelites and had taken many of them away into exile. So Daniel now was far from his homeland, but he still prayed every day to the God of Israel.

Darius favored Daniel above his other officers, so they plotted how to turn the king against him. And they went to Darius, saying:

"O King, may you live forever! Hear us, we pray. Let it be the law in Babylon for the next thirty days that if any man prays to any god, or asks a blessing of anyone but Darius the King, he shall be thrown to the lions."

"You wish this? Why?"

"For the sake of your great name, O King. The people must honor YOU first above all."

"Very well, so be it."

And then, when the new law was put in writing—which meant it could not be changed, even by the king himself—Daniel's enemies went to Darius, saying:

"O King, may you live forever! Your new law already has been broken. A man we know prayed to his God three times today. Shall he not be thrown to the lions?"

"Tell me his name."

"He is one of your officers."

"Tell me!"

"His name, O King, is—Daniel."

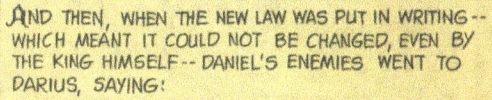

And Darius was troubled, for he did not want Daniel to die. So he searched for a way to save him, but there was no way—because the law was the law and no one could change it. When the sun went down, Darius sent men for Daniel, and they brought him to the edge of the deep pit that was the den of the lions. And Darius stood near the pit, and he said to Daniel:

"May your God save you from this death!"

And then his men threw Daniel down into the pit—and then they laid a stone over the mouth of the pit. Then Darius marked it with the King's seal, so that no man might dare to lift the stone and save Daniel.

Then the King went back to his palace, but he took no food that night, and he did not sleep. Instead, he mourned for Daniel. The next morning, he went to the mouth of the pit, and his men moved the stone, and the King cried out:

"Daniel—Daniel—was your God able to save you?"

"O King, may you live forever. Your servant is alive and well!"

King Darius was glad, and he ordered his men to lift Daniel out. And Daniel said:

"God sent His angel to shut the lions' mouth, because in His eyes I had done no wrong."

"And you have done no wrong in MY eyes, Daniel. But the new law is wrong—and I cast it out."

Then King Darius wrote to all peoples and all the nations, saying:

"THIS shall be the law in my lands—that men shall bow their heads before the God of Daniel, for HE is the living God, enduring for ever, and HIS kingdom and power shall never end!"

THE FIRST CHRISTMAS

NEARLY TWO THOUSAND YEARS AGO, WHEN THE ROMANS RULED OVER THE HOLY LAND, AN ORDER WENT FORTH FROM THE EMPEROR TO ALL THE PEOPLE:

"RISE UP FROM YOUR HOME PLACE, AND GO TO THE CITY OR TOWN WHERE YOUR FATHERS LIVED LONG AGO, AND THERE GIVE YOUR NAME TO MY OFFICERS, THAT YOU MAY BE NUMBERED AMONG MY SUBJECTS AND PAY TAXES TO ROME."

NOW THIS ORDER WAS CARRIED TO NAZARETH, IN A PART OF THE COUNTRY THAT WAS CALLED GALILEE. AND JOSEPH LIVED IN NAZARETH, WITH HIS WIFE MARY, WHO WAS EXPECTING A CHILD. AND HE SAID TO HER:

"WE MUST GO UP TO BETHLEHEM, THE CITY OF DAVID, BECAUSE I AM OF THE HOUSE OF DAVID, AS WERE ALL MY FATHERS BEFORE ME, BACK THROUGH TIME TO DAVID THE KING."

"JOSEPH -- MUST I GO WITH YOU?"

"YES. EVERYONE MUST BE NUMBERED."

"BUT MY BABY IS TO BE BORN SOON-- VERY SOON. TO MAKE A JOURNEY NOW MIGHT NOT BE GOOD FOR THE CHILD."

"WE WILL TAKE CARE-- BUT WE MUST GO, MARY. THE EMPEROR HAS ORDERED IT."

AND SO THEY SET OUT FROM NAZARETH. BUT TO SPARE MARY'S STRENGTH, THEY JOURNEYED ONLY A FEW MILES EACH DAY. AT LAST THEY REACHED BETHLEHEM, AND MARY SAID:

"MY BABY WILL BE BORN TONIGHT. YOU MUST FIND US A PLACE TO STAY."

AND JOSEPH WENT TO THE INN, BUT OTHERS HAD COME BEFORE THEM, AND THERE WAS NO ROOM NOW. THERE WAS ONLY ONE PLACE THEY COULD STAY-- THE STABLE OF THE INN.

AND THERE IT WAS -- IN THE STABLE THAT NIGHT -- THAT MARY'S BABY WAS BORN. AND SHE WRAPPED HIM IN SWADDLING CLOTHES, AND -- BECAUSE SHE HAD NO CRADLE FOR HIM -- SHE LAID HIM IN THE MANGER FROM WHICH THE ANIMALS ATE THEIR FOOD.

NOW, OUT IN THE FIELD AROUND BETHLEHEM, THERE WERE SHEPHERDS ON GUARD OVER THEIR FLOCKS. AND SUDDENLY AN ANGEL OF THE LORD STOOD BEFORE THEM --

--AND THE GLORY OF THE LORD SHONE ALL AROUND THEM, AND THE SHEPHERDS WERE FILLED WITH FEAR. BUT THE ANGEL SAID:

"BE NOT AFRAID-- FOR I BRING YOU GOOD NEWS OF GREAT JOY TO ALL PEOPLE. A SAVIOUR HAS BEEN BORN TO YOU TONIGHT IN THE CITY OF DAVID-- CHRIST, THE LORD!"

AND THEN THE SKIES WERE FILLED WITH ANGELS, ALL PRAISING GOD AND SAYING:

"GLORY TO GOD IN HEAVEN-- AND ON EARTH PEACE, GOODWILL AMONG MEN!"

THE THREE WISE MEN

Now when Jesus was born at Bethlehem, a new star was seen in the eastern sky. And sometime later, wise men from a far country came to Jerusalem, saying:

"Where is the child who was born to be king of the Jews? We saw his star rising in the east, and have come to worship him."

The words of the wise men were carried to King Herod, who ruled the land with the permission of Rome... The Romans were the real rulers. Now Herod wanted to remain king and not give way to anyone else. So he sent for the chief priests, and asked them:

"Where is the Messiah, the Christ, to be born?"

"In Bethlehem, O king. For it is written, 'Out of Bethlehem shall come a ruler who will govern my people of Israel.'"

Then King Herod sent for the wise men, and they told him they had seen the new star in the skies of their own country for the first time two years before and then they said:

"The star has led us all the way to this land... to find the child, that we may worship him. Do you, O king, know where he may be?"

"In Bethlehem, they say. Go -- search him out -- and when you have found him, bring me word, that I too may go and worship him."

The wise men set out from Jerusalem, and the star they had seen in the east went before them, and they followed it to Bethlehem. And the star came to rest over the house where the child was. The wise men cried out with joy, and they went into the house with the gifts they had brought from their country. And when they saw him -- when they saw the child lying near Mary his mother -- they fell on their knees before him, and bowed their heads to the new-born king. Then they opened their treasure-chests, and laid out their gifts before him -- gold, and sweet-smelling frankincense, and myrrh.

Then the wise men left Bethlehem, to return to their own land. But they did not stop at Jerusalem, for a dream warned them to say nothing to King Herod.

When the wise men had gone, an angel of the Lord came to Joseph, the husband of Mary, where he lay sleeping, and the angel said:

"Rise up -- and take the child and his mother, and flee with them into Egypt, and stay there until I tell you. For Herod is about to search for the child, to kill him."

So Joseph rose up, and set out that night with the child and Mary, his mother, and they made their way safely into Egypt.

They stayed there until Herod died. Then, at God's order, they came back to their homeland and settled at Nazareth, in Galilee. And there Jesus lived with Mary and Joseph, until it was time for him to begin his great work.

THE GOOD SAMARITAN

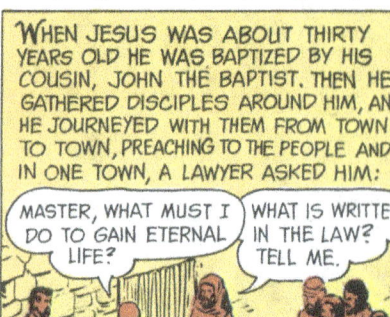

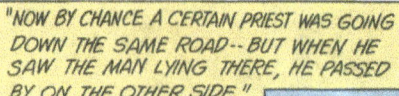

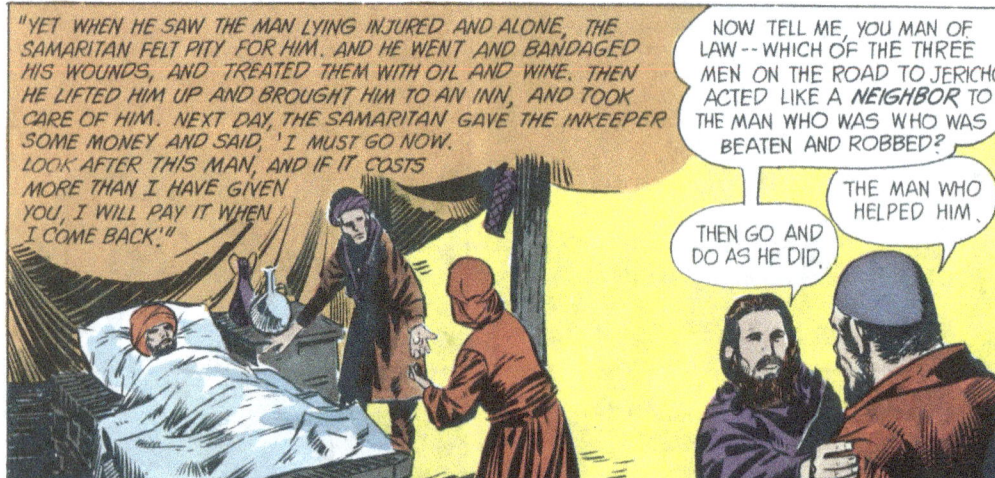

THE PRODIGAL SON

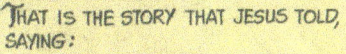

THE CRUCIFIXION

Jesus preached for three years and in that time he made many friends throughout the land. They believed that he was the son of God, and that God had sent him as the Messiah, the Christ, to redeem Israel and all the world.

But Jesus also made enemies. Some thought him a false prophet who was leading the people away from the law of Moses and God.

Jesus went up to Jerusalem with his disciples for the Passover, the feast that marks the day God saved the people of Israel from their taskmasters in Egypt.

He was accused of calling himself King of the Jews and arousing the people against the rule of Rome. And he was arrested and brought before Pontius Pilate, the Roman governor. Only Pilate could order a man to be put to death as a rebel -- and he did.

Then the Roman soldiers led Jesus away to Golgotha, the hill outside the city where men were put to death on the cross.

THE ASCENSION and The Pentecost

On the third day after he was crucified, Jesus rose from the dead. And that very day he showed himself to Mary of Magdala as she searched the tomb for his body. And he showed himself to Cleopas and his companions on the road to Emmaus seven miles from Jerusalem. And over the next forty days he showed himself to his disciples in Jerusalem and at the Sea of Galilee.

Soon after he first rose up, the disciples were gathered together, talking about this great wonder -- when suddenly Jesus stood there among them! They shook with fear, because they thought him a ghost. But Jesus said:

"Look at my hands and feet -- touch me -- I am really here. No ghost has flesh and bones as I have."

But the disciples still could not believe their eyes, much as they wanted to. So Jesus said to them:

"Have you anything here to eat?"

Then they gave him a piece of broiled fish, and he took it and ate it in front of them. Then Jesus spoke to them, explaining what was written about his coming. And he said:

"This is what it means, that the Christ was to suffer and then rise from the dead -- and that repentance and forgiveness of sins should be preached in his name to all nations. I shall send my Father's gift upon you. John, as you know, baptized with water -- but you will be baptized with the Holy Spirit. So stay here in this city until you have been given the power from on high. Then you shall bear witness for me in Jerusalem, and all over this land, and to the ends of the earth."

Then Jesus led his disciples up to the top of the Mount of Olives, and blessed them. And as they watched, Jesus was lifted up, and a cloud carried him out of their sight. And as he rose up to heaven and they stared after him -- suddenly two men robed in white stood with them, saying:

"Men of Galilee, why stand here looking up at the sky? Jesus, who has been taken away up to heaven, will come again -- the same way you saw him go!"

Forty days after the first Easter Sunday, the disciples of Jesus were gathered in a house in Jerusalem -- when suddenly there came from the sky a sound like a strong, driving wind -- and it filled the house -- and tongues like flames of fire appeared in the room and rested on each of the disciples. And they were all filled with the Holy Spirit and began to talk in other tongues -- and people out on the street heard them -- people who had come to Jerusalem from lands all over the earth -- and each was amazed to hear, in his own language, word of the great things God had done. And they said to Peter and the apostles:

"Tell us -- what are we to do?"

And Peter said to them:

"Repent and be baptized, every one of you, in the name of Jesus the Messiah for the forgiveness of your sins -- and you will receive the gift of the Holy Spirit. For the promise is to you, and to your children, and to all who are far away: Every one who invokes the name of the Lord shall be saved!"

www.ingramcontent.com/pod-product-compliance
Lightning Source LLC
Chambersburg PA
CBHW051215290426
44109CB00021B/2469